*The Widow's Son
and the Lost Word*

The Widow's Son and the Lost Word

Ramesh Gupta

Foreword by Robert Lomas

RESOURCE *Publications* · Eugene, Oregon

THE WIDOW'S SON AND THE LOST WORD

Copyright © 2022 Ramesh Gupta. All rights reserved. Except for brief quotations in critical publications or reviews, no part of this book may be reproduced in any manner without prior written permission from the publisher. Write: Permissions, Wipf and Stock Publishers, 199 W. 8th Ave., Suite 3, Eugene, OR 97401.

Resource Publications
An Imprint of Wipf and Stock Publishers
199 W. 8th Ave., Suite 3
Eugene, OR 97401

www.wipfandstock.com

PAPERBACK ISBN: 978-1-6667-3090-6
HARDCOVER ISBN: 978-1-6667-2293-2
EBOOK ISBN: 978-1-6667-2294-9

FEBRUARY 25, 2022

The Widow's Son and the Lost Word

is dedicated to my father

DHARM PAUL GUPTA

a life member of

Lodge Luce Abbey, No. 689

Scottish Constitution

Contents

Foreword by Robert Lomas   xi

Author's Note   xvii

The Widow's Son and the Lost Word

The Gathering of the Brethren	1
King Salomon's Dream	3
King Salomon Prospers	5
King Salomon Sends for King Hiram	7
King Salomon Seeks Hiram Abiff	9
Hiram Abiff's Reply	11
King Salomon's Messenger Departs	13
King Salomon Greets His Messenger	14
The People and King Salomon Sing	15
Salomon Enquires of Hiram Abiff	16
The Messenger's Reply	17
The Messenger's Sorrow	19

Hiram Abiff's Gift for King Salomon	21
King Hiram Arrives in Jerusalem	23
King Hiram's Gifts for King Salomon	24
Hiram Abiff's Prayer	26
The Building of the Temple Begins	28
Two Great Pillars	29
Three Ruffians of the Fellow Craft	30
Queen Balkis of Sheba	31
King Salomon Greets Balkis	33
Queen Balkis' Demand	35
King Salomon's Request	37
Balkis Accepts Salomon's Invitation	38
A Royal Agreement	41
King Salomon's Lust Prevails	43
The Building of the Temple	45
Hiram Abiff Answers Balkis' Command	47
Balkis Conspires to Kill the Architect	51
Balkis Calls the Three Ruffians	52
The Three Ruffians Conspire	54
The Three Ruffians Seek the Architect	56
Hiram Abiff Answers the Three Ruffians	58

The Three Ruffians Depart	60
The Brazen Sea	62
Balkis Resolves to Kill the Widow's Son	64
Balkis Calls the Three Ruffians Again	65
The Fellow Craft Recant	67
The Fellow Craft Inform King Salomon	68
Hiram Abiff Prays	69
Hiram Abiff's Final Prayer	71
The Heinous Deed is Done	74
The Widow's Son is Dead	79
A Sprig of Acacia	81
Confusion at the Temple	82
King Salomon Fears for the Widow's Son	84
King Salomon Orders a Search	86
The Three Ruffians Flee	87
The Self-Imposed Penalties	90
The Ruffians Captured	92
Mount Moriah's Secret	94
The Widow's Son Discovered	96
Attempts to Raise the Widow's Son	98
Punishment for the Guilty	100

Foreword

An interesting Poetic Enterprise to tell an Ancient story using an even older method of Storytelling.

THE OLDEST HUMAN STORY we know is about 5,000 years old. It was scratched onto a series of soft clay tablets which had then been baked hard. These tablets survived in the ruins of the Library of Ashurbanipal in the Assyrian city of Nineveh, where they were excavated by archaeologist Hormuzd Rassam in 1853. When they were deciphered from the long dead Sumerian language, they told a rip-roaring tale of the adventures of an ancient king of the biblical city of Ur. The storyline of *The Epic of Gilgamesh* is interesting but the method of storytelling is more fascinating. This wonderful tale was told in carefully structured stanzas of poetry. Nobody is quite sure how the original Sumerian sounded when spoken aloud, but Robert Temple, after studying the pattern of the Sumerian syllables, did a poetic translation into English in 1991. He called his epic, *He Who Saw Everything,* and captured the rhythm and drive of the story in beautiful English quatrain verse.

The story Ramesh Gupta tells in this book claims only to be 2,978 years old but is a myth which has been told, retold, and embellished by Freemasons who have handed it down behind the closed and guarded doors of their lodges for hundreds of years. Now you too can share in the wonder of this astonishing myth.

Foreword

To share his poetic retelling of this ancient Masonic myth, Ramesh Gupta, uses the poetic discipline of a quatrain structure. The story he retells is ancient, but his storytelling technique is even older than the parable. He makes the spoken words sing and resonate in harmony with the events he describes. To enjoy this book in full you should either read it out loud or bribe a competent and sympathetic reciter to read it to you. As the words sound out you will recognise the quatrain speech rhythms we all learned at our mother's knee. Most nursery rhymes are written in this form. Read aloud this simple example and hear the bouncy emotion take over your voice.

> Hey, diddle diddle, the cat and the fiddle.
> The cow jumped over the moon.
> The little dog laughed to see such fun.
> And the dish ran away with the spoon.

This little nonsense narrative is driven by a strong rhythmic beat in the words and some simple internal rhymes to punctuate that pulse (diddle, fiddle – moon, spoon). Its structure was burnt into your brain as a child by joyful repetition.

Ramesh Gupta is a man who understands the rhythms of the spoken word. He was brought up and educated in Scotland so learned the works of Robbie Burns, Alasdair mac Mhaighstir and Walter Scott. And from conversation with him I know he enjoys the classic excitement of Beowulf, the romantic sonnets of Shakespeare and the sweeping poetic inspiration of the Vedas and the Upanishads.

He has taken the time to study the twelfth century Middle Welsh works of *Y Mabinogion* and the poems of Dayffd ap Gwilym. He has listened and admired the complex structures of Cynghanedd verse (Cynghanedd is a Welsh poetic protocol that uses alliteration and internal rhyme in a classic form that is subject to competitive testing in the poetry competitions of the Eisteddfod). Cynghanedd was formally codified at the Caerwys Eisteddfod of 1523 into four basic types, and using them a skilful bard, such as Ramesh, can convey an infinite variety of subtle effects. As

Foreword

I listened to myself reading out the stanzas of his epic I couldn't help but notice that Ramesh listened carefully to the resonances of that most popular cynghanedd form, known as the Englyn.

Let me declare in interest. As well as being fascinated by the ritual and purpose of Freemasonry, I am also a great fan of the Welsh Victorian poet and novelist Daniel Owen of Mold, Flintshire, who wrote only in Welsh. Since I retired from Bradford University, I have been steadily translating and publishing Daniel's work into English (see *Rhys Lewis* and *Ten Nights in the Black Lion*).

For a recent St David's Day meeting at a Welsh Masonic Lodge, I translated one of Daniel's cynghanedd poems using Englyn quatrain stanzas. It is called *The Morning Star*. It is difficult to capture meaning when rendering a poem from one language into another. But to comply with the syllable count and the rhyming sequence of the Englyn protocol makes the task much harder. Here is the first verse in Daniel's Welsh and my English version.

> Y Seren fore—brydferth em!
> Mae 'th lachar wedd a'th hawddgar drem,
> Fel angel Duw yn rhoddi tro
> Hyd uchel gànt y nefoedd fawr,
> Gan ddyfal syllu tua ,r llawr,
> I edrych aeth rhyw fyd ar ffo!

Now my English translation following the same cynghanedd structure.

> Oh, beautiful bright morning Star!
> Shines your light and comely aspect far,
> Like God's great angel peering down
> From heaven's high hundreds you astound,
> To look with candour at the ground,
> And see how passing days are flown!

It took a lot of effort to capture the meaning and still conform to the cynghanedd, and my version is clumsy compared to the fluid eloquence of the original. And that is only one stanza.

Ramesh Gupta has taken a rich and complex story and told it in 445 quatrains. Each quatrain follows the Englyn pattern of a strict metre of syllable counts to give a rhythm which is echoed on the syllables of all three lines. The part of the first line after alliterates with the first part of the second line and the second and fourth lines end in a rhyme. Here is an example taken from, "The Widow's Son and the Lost Word".

> The Lord looked down upon the land,
> as so often now He would.
> And seeing the Brethren gathered there,
> He saw that all was good.

This classic four-line Englyn stanza conveys the poet's narrative thrust through a happy set of rhythmic word sounds which are a pleasure to read aloud. The tale unfolds through fifty-five episodes split into 445 carefully crafted quatrains.

But enough praise for the subtle bardic craft of Ramesh Gupta. Let me now say something about his choice of subject.

Freemasonry is the oldest secular, philosophical, self-help society in the Western world. Since the mid fifteenth century it has been using three great principles, Brotherly Love, Relief and Truth, to teach its Initiates how to understand themselves, their place in society and the purpose of their lives. Freemasonry describes itself as a, "peculiar system of morality, veiled in allegory and illuminated by symbols". One of its main methods of passing on its knowledge is to perform ritual plays within the lodge which tell moral stories from the past. One important story it tells is about the building of King Salomon's Temple, and the events which happened during that construction—how Salomon choose as his chief architect a widow's son who knew all the secrets of how to build and what happened during the construction of the most beautiful building the world has ever known.

Ramesh Gupta has applied all his Masonic insight and using his Bardic craft has written a traditional epic poem which tells the myth of the building of the Temple in graphic and gripping detail.

If you are a Freemason you will learn much background material to the Third Degree, and if you are not a Freemason you

Foreword

will enjoy the powerful themes of this popular Masonic myth presented with equally powerful perception and elegiac charm.

ROBERT LOMAS

Author's Note

"The Widow's Son" needs no introduction to those who are familiar with the Old Testament story as related in the books of Joshua, Judges, Samuel and Kings. To those readers who are Freemasons, Hiram Abiff stands as a veritable colossus, the most significant personage to grace his and their time. His commitment to the building of King Salomon's Temple and his selfless sacrifice mirrors and foretells the redemption of Mankind a thousand years in the future and speaks to us through the ages of something far, far greater, stronger and more beautiful than we can yet hope to fully appreciate.

The writing of, "The Widow's Son" sprang from an appreciation of the power and a love of the poetry of the Scottish Masonic Third degree. No other form of communication has so touched my heart and my soul. The masonic story however, is in many ways, rather different to its Old Testament counterpart, the reasons having long eluded human memory, lying lost in the sands of the desert and in the mists of time. In the masonic version, the Temple remains incomplete, unlike the Old Testament narrative in which the building is not only completed but stands as a mighty edifice, a resting place for the Most High and the Ark of the Covenant, as well as a testament to the glory of its architect and builders.

The account presented in this version of the story rests largely but not exclusively nor entirely on the Scottish Masonic, Master Mason degree. In addition to the basic masonic narrative, it incorporates elements of the Old Testament story. Moreover, it has

Author's Note

absorbed myth and legend that has been passed down over the millennia. It also has embedded within it, a kernel of what I believe to be a Universal Truth – that the lost word will be restored to us by the Most High if we embrace the tenets espoused by the Craft.

It is my earnest hope that the cement of Brotherly love and Craft principles continue to bind and guide Freemasons the world over and that they will someday be embraced by all Humankind. Through this simple act, the metaphorical Temple shall be completed and the ineffable name of the Most High will be ours again.

In its own way, I hope that this retelling of, "The Widow's Son and the Lost Word" will make some meaningful contribution towards that end.

Ramesh Gupta
March 2021

The Gathering of the Brethren

The Lord looked down upon the land,
    as so often now He would.
And seeing the Brethren gathered there,
    He saw that all was good.

For the time of war was ended;
    the killing now was o'er.
The Lord's Heart swelled with pride;
    how could He love them more?

'Though David was a mighty King,
    and belovèd of the Lord,
yet he could not build the Temple,
    for he lived by the sword.

"My House shall be a house of peace,
    for each and every man,
and I shall dwell with my people here,
    in harmony in this land.

"This shall be a House of Rest,
    for the Ark of my Covenant.
And I shall dwell with the Law therein,
    where my people may give thanks.

"David's son now is King;
    the leader of this land.
And I shall lead the Brethren,
    and guide them with Mine Hand.

"So let the building now begin,
    My Temple soon shall stand,
amongst the Brethren gathered here,
    in this Good and Holy Land."

King Salomon's Dream

So the Lord appeared in a dream,
    to Salomon, David's son,
and told him of the Temple,
    whose building must soon be done.

"I shall grant to thee one boon,
    for I do favour thee.
And if thou dost remain true,
    I shall set thine spirit free."

"Oh Lord! Oh Lord, my Only God,
    pray glory be to Thee.
For thou hast granted me a crown,
    and more hast Thou given me.

"That I have Thee by my side,
    is all happiness for me.
Pray guide me in this choice,
    that I serve only Thee.

"I am yet young of years,
    and not worthy to be King.
So aid me in this matter,
    that I may Thine Glory sing."

"Ask of Me yet anything,
    for thou art My David's son.
And if thou wilt harken to My Voice,
    great deeds by thee shall be done.

"So ask now for thy gift,
    and I shall grant it thee.
But take thou care o'er this task,
    before thou ask it of Me."

King Salomon Prospers

"My Lord, my God, Almighty One,
    I ask the righteous way.
That I may rule with compassion,
    my people each night and day."

The Lord smiled to hear these words,
    granting wisdom to Salomon.
And riches also He gave to him,
    His David's wisest son.

The people grew from strength to strength,
    ruled by a wise King.
Peace and prosperity also they knew,
    in the Lord's Care, lacking nothing.

So Salomon thought to thank the Lord,
    and to Him a song did sing.
"Oh Lord, my God, my Only One,
    I thank Thee for this ruler's ring.

"And for more than this I thank Thee;
    for the Goodness Thou did bestow.
For Thou hast granted all to me,
    and laid mine enemies low.

"So I shall build to Thee Thy Temple,
    wherein I shall sing Thine Praise.
And I shall not lift my hands in anger,
    but in prayer to Thee them raise."

The Lord was pleased to hear these words,
and blessed the King of that land,
inspiring the building of the Temple,
and giving strength to his hand.

King Salomon Sends for King Hiram

And King Salomon sent out word,
    to King Hiram his trusted friend.
A message to him was writ,
    and across the land was sent.

"Worthy brother of good report,
    my loyal and worthy friend,
truly have I need of thee;
    thy skill, I pray, me lend.

"For the Lord my God has granted me,
    a holy vision it seems.
So I must build His Temple,
    as I beheld it in my dream.

"The Lord my God has given me,
    a wise, discerning heart.
And so I call to thee my friend,
    as thou hast been from the start.

"Come aid me at this time,
    for a Temple I must build.
And within its marble pillars and walls,
    with all riches I shall it fill.

"Delay thou not in coming here,
    for I have such need of thee.
And in this time of plenty and peace,
    pray render aid to me.

"Spare no task nor any means,
    by which to come to my land.
And we two shall commence this task,
    by the power of God's Great Hand.

"And I shall reward thee well my friend,
    and all whom thou shalt bring.
And when the task is o'er and done,
    to the Lord we both shall sing.

"And one more brother I shall enlist,
    to aid us in this matter.
And with his help, the Temple build,
    and thus complete the latter.

"So my friend, my Worthy Brother,
    come from the Kingdom of Tyre.
Come and sit with me this day,
    and prepare the Holy Fire."

And swiftly then the message went,
    o'er land, air and sea,
that Hiram, King of Tyre might come,
    and the Lord's Temple be.

King Salomon Seeks Hiram Abiff

And another message Salomon sent,
    to an Architect of old.
To the Widow's Son, Hiram Abiff,
    this message too was told.

"My Lord the Worthy Salomon,
    has commanded this of me.
For I am but his messenger,
    whom he has sent to thee.

"The Lord our God is with our King,
    restoring peace to our land.
And wealth, power and wisdom too,
    He has given to Salomon's hand.

"In a dream did our God appear,
    to our noble King so wise.
And there in Devine Sleep,
    a vision came to his eyes.

"And our Lord God did speak to him,
    'though He did not reveal His Face.
And there in that noble sleep,
    did our God King Salomon grace.

"The vision was of a mighty Temple,
    whose like has ne'er been seen.
And it was the most beautiful place,
    whose like has ne'er yet been.

"For it was built of the finest stone,
    that e'er did grace our land.
And our Lord God did place this task,
    into our noble King's hand.

"And the building shone as a mighty beacon,
    to clear the darkest night.
And like the desert cloud by day,
    it shone with Devine Light.

"So my noble Lord bids me,
    to enlist thy honourable aid.
To build a Temple to our God,
    'ere its memory does fade.

"Pray tell me now, 'ere I depart,
    what shall be thine reply.
Wilt thou assist our noble King,
    that I might to him fly?"

Hiram Abiff's Reply

"Kind brother," said the Widow's Son,
    "thou art a faithful man.
And I shall give thee my reply,
    in this my Mother Land.

"The Lord thy God is known to me,
    for I too serve Him.
And with His Aid in all my trials,
    did I each battle win.

"The Truth you bear, 'tis plain to see,
    and I must render aid.
For the Lord our God's Memory,
    from my heart shall ne'er fade.

"So let me put thy heart at ease,
    and give thee my reply,
that thou might be on thy way,
    and to King Salomon fly.

"I shall gladly leave my Mother land,
    and depart from my belovèd mother.
And I shall aid thee in this task,
    'though I have no father, or brother.

"For I know the Lord will provide,
    all my mother does need.
I need not have a heavy heart,
    for He shall her shelter and feed.

"But this I pray thee, remain a while,
    and give thy body rest.
My mother and I shall tend to thee,
    'ere thou fulfil the King's request."

King Salomon's messenger then did dance,
    to hear the goodly reply.
And he there praised the Lord his God,
    that to his King he might fly.

King Salomon's Messenger Departs

"Good Sir, I cannot tarry,
    for I must hurry home.
For my noble Lord does wait for me,
    in his palace quite alone.

"The King commands I return at once,
    on this good and noble day.
And so I take my leave of thee,
    for no longer should I stay."

And so the messenger took his leave,
    and hurried on his way.
He traveled with all possible haste,
    tarrying not through night or day.

And when he did at home arrive,
    he came to his Noble King.
And on humble, bended knee there,
    he kissed the Royal Ring.

King Salomon Greets His Messenger

"My good and faithful messenger,
    I pray thee speak to me.
For these many long days and nights,
    I have awaited thee.

"Tell me of the King of Tyre,
    that good and faithful man.
Will he come to aid thy King,
    in this God's chosen Land?"

"My Lord, my Lord, my noble King,
    the news is great and good.
For King Hiram will aid thee here,
    as thou said he surely would.

"Thy request he did so well receive,
    with joy so great to behold.
And so he sends this gift to thee,
    of silver and of gold."

And the messenger then delivered there,
    the gifts of Hiram the King.
Gold and silver which sun-like shone,
    and his very own Royal ring.

And all the court did marvel there,
    to see the wealth of Kings.
And so moved were they all,
    as one they began to sing.

The People and King Salomon Sing

"Praise be to our Lord and God,
    for He is Truth and Light.
And He will be with us now,
    through all our darkest nights."

And Salomon too did homage,
    by lifting up his voice.
And there amongst his cherished people,
    he stood and did rejoice.

"Oh Lord, my God of Israel,
    Thou art Good and Kind.
For Thou hast given Fraternal Love,
    which shall all men bind.

"And for this too I thank Thee now,
    King Hiram, my trusty friend.
And I shall sing to Thee Thy Praise,
    until my life does end."

And once more turning to his man,
    King Salomon bade him rise.
And as he took him by the hand,
    he looked into his eyes.

Salomon Enquires of Hiram Abiff

"My good and faithful servant,
    tell me more I pray.
What of the Architect so fair,
    what has thou to say?

"I know his skill of many years long,
    and fair is the work of his hands.
Will he too render aid,
    in this my Mother Land?

"He is industrious and wise,
    and a builder of great fame.
And all the nations of the earth,
    do know his goodly name.

"He is a Master Mason,
    who works with jewels and gold.
And I must receive him here,
    if I am to save my soul.

"So pray my Brother, hear my prayer,
    and tell news of this man.
Is he still the greatest builder,
    in this or any land?"

And then the messenger's eyes did close,
    as he looked down to the ground.
And tears welled up from his heart
    in that silence all around.

The Messenger's Reply

"My Lord, my Lord, thou mighty King,
    my heart is torn apart.
For Hiram Abiff will come to thee,
    that thy work may soon start."

Then Salomon did once more rejoice,
    and knelt in solemn prayer.
And his people too were silent then,
    as they prayed into the air.

Then again King Salomon arose,
    with his hand upon his ring.
And with his people gathered there,
    to the Lord God he did sing.

"Oh Lord, my God, I praise Thee still,
    and kneel on bended knee.
Hear this my simple song of joy,
    which I offer unto Thee."

And all the people sang again,
    all but only one.
The King's good messenger wept and wept,
    until the song was done.

Then Salomon beheld this sight,
    and looked towards the man.
For he alone did not sing,
    in all that good land.

"Why dost thou weep to speak such news,
    'tis tidings surely good?
Wilt not thou join with us in song,
    as all Good Men now should?

"But this, methinks, is somewhat amiss,
    that thou shouldst weep here so?
What pray, has befallen thee,
    that thine heart is laid so low?"

The Messenger's Sorrow

The messenger brushed his tears aside;
    at King Salomon he gazed.
And as his heart did almost break,
    in his hands he placed his face.

"My Noble Lord, thou art so kind,
    thou carest so for me.
For I dare not tell the news I have,
    Hiram Abiff would tell thee.

"For my heart is heavy indeed,
    to tell thee sad news so.
And it is for this Goodly Man,
    that my heart is laid so low.

"The Lord our God is Omnipotent;
    all knowledge belongs to He.
But Hiram Abiff's father is dead,
    and taken away from thee.

"And so my heart does sorely grieve,
    for the Widow's only Son.
But still he bids me tell to thee,
    at thine command he does come.

"He gave no thought but for our God,
    who has touched his heart and head.
And so I grieve for the Widow's Son,
    for his brothers too are dead.

"The Lord our God did appear to him,
   in a dream as He did to thee.
And this is all he has to give -
   his token of his fidelity."

Hiram Abiff's Gift for King Salomon

The messenger stretched forth his hand,
    and gave to Salomon a gift.
And the King too fell to his knees,
    as the gift he did kiss.

"My Lord and God, Omnipotent One,
    how Wise and Great Thou art.
For compassion Thou hast given me,
    and a wise, discerning heart.

"This act alone is known to Thee,
    that Thou take these people so.
For Thou hast released their very souls,
    that to Heaven they did go.

"But the Widow now is left alone,
    with her one and only son.
And he too Thou hast given me,
    that Thy Work may soon be done.

"Pray guard this Widow and her son,
    and I shall receive them here.
For she shall be my mother too,
    that I may have her near.

"For Hiram Abiff's only gift,
    I receive with his sad news,
and verily I shall treasure this,
    his mother's only shoe."

And so the people did honour them,
    the Widow and her son.
They waited in anticipation,
    each and every one.

King Hiram Arrives in Jerusalem

The days passed, the nights drew in,
    the people waited still.
And every one there did pray,
    to do the Lord's Will.

Then one day King Hiram arrived,
    when brightly shone the sun.
And King Salomon greeted him,
    with his people every one.

"I greet thee my foreign Brother,
    'tis good to see thee here.
For we have waited all these days,
    to have thee with us near.

"For now the plans can soon be drawn,
    whilst we await the Widow's Son.
And let us pray, Lord keep him safe,
    that His Will might soon be done."

"My worthy friend, King Salomon,
    I greet thee with a kiss.
And more I bring to aid thee here,
    that thou fulfil thy wish.

"I bring with me great men from Tyre,
    to aid thy Holy Task.
For I have not tarried one single day,
    as thou did of me ask."

King Hiram's Gifts for King Salomon

"I bring with me great, mighty cedars,
    and precious metals too.
For this Temple must glorify God
    with colours bright and new.

"So let us now make a start,
    and tarry here no more.
Join with me this day in prayer,
    as we have done so oft before.

"Oh justly Great and Mighty Lord,
    thy Ways are Good and True.
Pray aid us in this mighty task,
    that we might worship You.

"Give strength to men gathered here,
    and keenness of their eyes.
And guide us through Thy worthy Servant,
    King Salomon the Wise.

"Make fast our ways before Thee;
    free Thou the Cable Tow.
And let our thoughts be with Thee,
    as we work on earth below.

"Let these great and mighty cedars,
    adorn Thy Temple Walls.
And let these stones and metals too,
    light up Thy Temple Halls.

"And let this linen cover,
    the ground which is so cold.
That we may worship Thee,
    with all our hearts and souls."

And verily was Salomon pleased,
    to hear this worthy prayer.
And so he bowed in reverence,
    to his worthy friend so fair.

Hiram Abiff's Prayer

And so the work did then commence,
    beneath the sky and sun.
And thus the many men would work,
    until the work was done.

And so too did Hiram Abiff,
    the Widow's Worthy son.
He too did labour there,
    when all other men had gone.

On rising in the morning,
    he would greet the coming day.
And with a prayer to his Lord,
    these words he would say.

"Oh Mighty Lord, my God above,
    the day has now begun.
So guide this Thy servant here,
    the widow's humble son.

"For I must complete this task,
    that Thou appointed me.
And I shall ever be Thy Son
    that I might glorify Thee."

And also at the day's closing,
    at the dipping of the sun,
Hiram Abiff would once more pray,
    that his task might soon be done.

"Oh Mighty Lord, my God above,
    now is this day soon gone.
I pray Thee guide Thy humble Servant,
    that this task may soon be done."

And so upon the morrow,
    at the beginning of the day,
Hiram Abiff, the Architect,
    as ever he humbly prayed.

"Oh Lord, my God, my Only One,
    look down upon your man.
And let Thy Wisdom flow in him,
    in this King Salomon's land.

"For upon this day I shall begin,
    the task appointed me.
And I shall build a Wondrous Temple,
    for the glory of only Thee.

"And every day at High Twelve,
    I shall pray alone to Thee,
in preparation for the day ahead,
    and the task appointed me.

"And at the closing of each day,
    when others shall rest their heads,
I shall give thanks to thee alone,
    'ere I retire to my bed."

The Building of the Temple Begins

The King of Tyre and the many men,
    whom he did there command,
set to work upon the Temple,
    in that Good and Holy land.

Many cedars from Lebanon,
    and gold and jewels too,
were brought from far and distant lands,
    to praise the One God True.

Masons, men and carpenters,
    and so many other men,
toiled together beneath the sun -
    a unified lodge of Brethren.

Two Great Pillars

And as the days did by and go,
    and men did work together,
so the Temple was almost done,
    to keep safe the Word forever.

Two great pillars stood in front,
    built from finest brass.
And shone with the Lord's Glory,
    like myriad celestial stars.

And these two pillars were identified,
    by Hiram they were known.
And their names were kept secret,
    until the King was them shown.

Then like an arrow to a bow,
    as swiftly it would go,
the secret names were sent;
    to Master Masons known.

Three Ruffians of the Fellow Craft

And there outside the Architect,
    a brazen sea would make.
And so three ruffians did conspire,
    his life and soul to take.

For they were not entrusted,
    with the Sacred, Secret Skills,
to make them Master Masons,
    and so they would him kill.

But in this task they were aided,
    by a source that was no man.
And so for pious Hiram Abiff,
    his most earnest trial began.

Queen Balkis of Sheba

King Salomon's mighty wealth and store,
    were known throughout the land.
And of all he was the envy,
    of Queen, King and man.

And fame of Salomon's wisdom,
    went far across the land.
And so it came to Balkis,
    across a sea of sand.

And Balkis she did seek to know,
    the source of Wisdom True.
For she desired the King's true wealth,
    which was known to but few.

And so she journeyed many days,
    far from her sun-burned land.
And when King Salomon she did face,
    she offered him her hand.

And Salomon was speechless made,
    to behold this beauteous Queen.
For her beauty shone as she was known -
    the fairest ever seen.

"Oh mighty King, King Salomon,
    pray greet this humble maid.
For I have travelled far and wide."
    These words Balkis said.

"I have come to meet with thee,
    and learn thy Wisdom too.
And gain somewhat of the knowledge,
    of thy One God True."

King Salomon Greets Balkis

"Sweet Queen, thou maiden fair,
    I greet thee with mine hand.
Thy beauty is well know to me,
    and to all men in this land.

"And I King Salomon would ask,
    but one boon of thee.
Stay thou here in this land,
    ever near, beside me.

"'Though thou art from a foreign land,
    and worship other gods;
yet I would deny thee nought,
    for thou dost call me Lord."

Then Salamon spread forth his hand,
    and bade Queen Balkis come.
And his wisdom shone around,
    like rays from a golden sun.

A spill of water lay between,
    King Salomon and his guest.
And as Queen Balkis went to him,
    she raised her silken dress.

So gracefully she walked across,
    that shallow spill of water.
So lightly then she took his hand,
    Sheba's beautiful daughter.

But Salamon was astute and wise;
    his gaze was on the mirror
of the shallow spill of water,
    reflecting like a river.

'Though beautiful and gracefully,
    walked Sheba's lovely daughter,
her long legs slim, and smooth of skin,
    she did not touch the water!

The colours of her flowing dress,
    of finest silk were woven.
But the sandals that she wore,
    revealed both feet were cloven!

Queen Balkis' Demand

"Lord, 'tis true I call thee here,
    for that is what thou art.
And I am lost to thee alone,
    to thee I give mine heart.

"Yet shall I not lie with thee,
    for to me it is a sin,
that any man should thus lie,
    a woman's body within.

"One boon more I ask of thee,
    to set my heart at peace.
That I might tarry here a while,
    'till my thirst for knowledge cease.

"For thy wisdom is known to all,
    across the great divide.
And I have travelled these many days,
    that I might with thee abide.

"I have come to see myself,
    the great and noble King.
I have come to meet with thee,
    of whom the land does sing."

"Beauty great is thine 'tis true,"
    King Salomon then he said.
"And I do now understand-
    the question in thine head.

"The Lord, my God, He is but One,
    the only God above.
His name is ever on my lips;
    for 'tis Him alone I love.

"He instructs me with this mighty task,
    the Holy Ark to keep.
And I shall ever do His Will,
    for 'tis Him that I seek.

"I have built a Mighty Temple,
    in which the Ark might rest.
And also serve to worship Him,
    whom I love above all else.

"My father David did establish,
    rule in this God's land.
And the Ark was given unto him,
    delivered into his hand.

"But now the task is mine to keep,
    the Ark from all harm.
And so inside this Mighty Place,
    shall it weather every storm."

King Salomon's Request

"But for some time, pray tarry here,
    be thou my worthy guest.
And in the sanctuary of this palace,
    grant thy body rest.

"Go prepare thyself this evening,
    with me for to dine.
And I shall prepare goodly food,
    and the very best of wine.

"Nothing shall be spared for thee -
    a feast of the finest food.
And thou shalt know the Simple Truth,
    that the Lord my God is Good."

Balkis Accepts Salomon's Invitation

"My Lord, my Lord," said Queen Balkis.
    "I know thou art most kind.
And I and these my servants here,
    did indeed a wise King find.

"So I shall this evening dine with thee,
    and rest with thee this night.
And so I shall prepare myself,
    whilst yet there is some light.

"And when our evening meal is done,
    we shall both to bed.
But yet I shall not lie with thee,"
    Queen Balkis once more said.

But Salomon did look with lust,
    upon the beauteous Queen,
for truly she was the fairest,
    he had ever, ever seen.

"Fair Balkis thou art fair indeed,
    more fair than any here.
And I must confess this to thee,
    this night I would have thee near.

"So lie, this night, with me I pray,
    and be my foremost Queen.
And I shall make thee more powerful,
    than any man has seen.

"So let us now dine this night,
    then let us both to bed.
There shall we two be one,"
    King Salomon to her said.

"My Lord and King thou art 'tis true -
    yet this cannot be!
For I am no Queen of thine,
    and cannot thus lie with thee.

"So let us eat our fill this night,
    beneath the starry sky.
And then in our separate beds,
    we two alone must lie."

But deep within King Salomon,
    there arose a flaming fire.
He knew he would not rest that night,
    so great was his desire.

"Balkis, tonight night lie with me,
    and let us be as one.
And on the morrow shall we two,
    greet the morning sun.

"For we two shall rule as one,
    this and thy land too.
Yes, you shall be my foremost Queen.
    Pray hear my words true.

"But shouldst thou deny me this night,
    then shall I cast thee aside.
For thou shalt then my prisoner be,
    thus shalt thou here abide."

A Royal Agreement

Then Balkis did turn to him,
    and looked him in the eye.
"This night shall I spend with thee,
    'though I shall not with thee lie."

So King Salomon prepared a feast,
    with food and wine the best.
And before the eating did commence,
    the meal was by the Lord blessed.

But all the food which Balkis ate,
    was highly spiced and dry.
And as the evening did progress,
    Salomon came to her nigh.

"My Queen, my Queen," Salomon said.
    "The moon is now on high.
Let us therefore now retire,
    and thou shalt with me lie."

"My Lord, my Lord, I beg of thee,
    to my head the wine has gone.
'Though thou wouldst know me this night,
    Pray let this not be done.

"Do not take me here by force;
    do not force thyself on me.
For if thou shouldst thus do,
    shall I forever hate thee."

Yet Salomon did try his hand,
    for he would not be deterred.
And so the beautiful Queen of Sheba,
    these words from him heard.

"My Queen, my Queen, sweet Balkis,
    I shall not so force thee.
But if thou take ought of value,
    thou shalt surely lie with me.

"Take from me whatever thou wilt,
    but first ask it of me.
And if thou ask it not of me,
    shall I avenge myself on thee.

"So come my Queen, with me this night -
    my chamber beckons there.
Come. Come my fairest Queen.
    Come rest my Balkis fair."

King Salomon's Lust Prevails

So they two did then retire,
    and to Salomon's chamber go.
But of all Salomon's Wisdom,
    poor Balkis did not yet know.

For he commanded of his servants,
    in his chamber leave some water.
There by the Queen's bed,
    beside Sheba's fairest daughter.

And there in the dead of night,
    Queen Balkis fell asleep.
And as she did sweetly dream,
    Salomon awake did keep.

And then not knowing what she did,
    Balkis stretched out her hand.
Water did she drink not knowing,
    she was watched by Salomon.

"Balkis now art thou mine!"
    Salomon then did say.
"So now thy promise to me keep,
    before the dawning of day."

"My Lord, my Lord! What dost thou say?"
    fair Balkis then she cried.
"'Tis but a little water,
    else of thirst I died.

"Surely thou wouldst not deny,
    thy guest and servant here,
but a drink of cool, clear water,
    from one who holds thee dear?"

"Ah Balkis, Balkis, thou art most fair,
    and sweet and innocent.
'Though God has granted thee beauty,
    wisdom He did not thee send.

"'Though gold and jewels I have,
    and material wealth so great,
yet has He given to me,
    mastery of thine fate.

"For what on earth is more precious,
    than the water of this land?
Save perhaps the Ark of God,
    and the goodness of God's Hand?

"So now thou must lie with me,
    and keep thy promise made.
Before the memory of that pledge,
    from thy mind does fade."

And so the Queen, fair Balkis,
    lay with Salomon that night.
And in the morning she did greet,
    the day's new, virgin light.

The Building of the Temple

The building of the Temple,
    continued on and on.
The Brethren daily worked and built,
    beneath the burning sun.

And 'though they toiled beneath the sun,
    with the noisy din around,
yet never once the Ark did hear,
    a single, solitary sound.

And every day at hot High Twelve,
    Hiram prayed to God above.
And nightly too he did the same,
    so great for God his love.

The pillars now complete stood tall;
    they shone clear in the sun.
And still the Brethren worked and toiled,
    until each day was done.

Balkis then to Salomon came,
    to view the winding stairs.
And so then did King Salomon,
    to the site take Balkis fair.

The Queen of Sheba then did meet,
    the Architect of fame.
And so virtuous was this man,
    she sought to know his name.

And Balkis in her heart conspired,
    to meet the Widow's Son.
And to her chamber late one night,
    the Architect she sumoned.

Hiram Abiff Answers Balkis' Command

"Fair Queen, in answer to Royal command,
    I come," said the Widow's Son.
"Even at this ungodly hour,
    now that my prayers are done.

"What service may I offer thee?
    What wouldst thou have me do?
For I shall do whate'er I can,
    'though to God I am true."

"Thy fame is like unto the King,
    'though thy mother has no husband.
News of the Temple and thee,
    are known throughout the land.

"Some say you hail from afar,
    a land beyond the sea.
Pray tell me who thy father is.
    Come, sit thee here by me.

"Still others here they say of thee,
    thou art a son of Dan,
imbued with secret knowledge;
    a cunning, worthy man.

"But perchance your father hails,
    from the very land of Tyre.
And the knowledge given thee,
    comes from the Most High.

"I would thou confide in me,
    the secret of thine Art.
Come, sit. Be my comfort here,
    tell me all in thine heart.

"It is said that the Lord thy God,
    is a mighty God indeed.
And if this is true I do not know,
    why the hungry He does not feed.

"And more than this I would ask of thee,
    of thy Lord God above.
And shouldst thou tell me thy secret,
    I shall give to thee my love.

"What knowledge here is known to thee,
    for this do I fear.
Such knowledge is great indeed.
    Wilst thou my questions hear?

"And of the Ark of the Covenant,
    tell me thou man of might.
For I would reward any man,
    who allowed me its sight."

"Fair Queen, I would tell thee all,
    of my Lord God above.
For above all else in Heaven or earth,
    'tis Him I serve and love.

"'Tis true I am a Master Mason;
    this is my working trade.
And 'though I have the secret knowledge,
    with the Lord a pledge I made.

"The Secrets of a Master Mason,
    shall be known to but three.
And 'though in time all Brothers shall know,
    these I cannot tell thee."

"Pray tell good Master, Hiram Abiff,
    thou may be the Widow's Son.
But of all the men in all the land,
    in love I would have but one.

"So look you here upon my body.
    Behold my smooth, soft skin.
Come lie this night with me,
    for love can be no sin."

"Fair Queen, most fair thou art,
    of all who are in this land.
So I pray thee now ask ought me—
    but ask not to stain my hand.

"Thy supple, left breast I see,
    thy right leg too is bare.
'Though thou art of the fairer sex,
    for such love I do not care.

"So pray now let me leave;
    I shall from thee depart.
And I shall keep the Mason's Word,
    in the repository of my heart.

"My heart does soar at the sight of thee,
    for my body is weak within.
Yet I shall to my Lord be true.
    With thee I shall not sin.

"For 'though I am a humble man,
    and not of Royal blood.
Yet I know of my lineage,
    traced beyond the Great Flood.

"'Though my forefather's soul is stained,
    with the blood of another,
yet shall I not betray my God,
    nor yet my Brethren Brothers."

And so the Architect did leave;
    he left Queen Balkis shamed.
Yet within her heart she pondered,
    the Widow's Son's name.

But her pride would not let her lie,
    for Hiram Abiff's injury.
She ever recalled his steadfast words,
    as men shall eternally.

Balkis Conspires to Kill the Architect

And so the building of the Temple,
    went ever on and on.
With gold and silver and works of brass,
    and mighty cedars from Lebanon.

And daily did the Queen of Sheba,
    see the Widow's Son.
And nightly did she think of him,
    when his work and prayers were done.

And once more she summoned him,
    to talk was her desire.
Perchance he would succumb,
    to her lust and passion's fire.

But once again she was to find,
    this was a pious man.
For he would not be tempted,
    like any other man.

And so she conspired to kill him,
    and end his noble line.
And called to her three Fellow Craft,
    and told them of her mind.

Balkis Calls the Three Ruffians

"Go call to me cunning Jubela,
    and Jubelo and Jubelum too.
For I have heard they are discontented,
    with this man so true!"

The Fellow Craft soon were called,
    and a wicked plan devised.
For the good Widow's only Son,
    would not with Balkis lie.

"Go ye now and gather men,
    and kill this pious man.
For he shall not refuse me and live,
    in this or any land.

"I care not how it is done,
    I care not this to know.
I care only for his Secret,
    that he would not to me show.

"He is a Master Mason.
    He is known through all the earth.
And the very mention of this man,
    fills righteous hearts with mirth.

"His Lord God has granted him,
    knowledge Wise and True.
And this alone he has told to me,
    shall be known to but a few.

"So kill him now, let it be done,
    and cast him into disgrace.
Let the deed soon be done,
    that I suffer no more his face!

"I know thee all Fellow Craft;
    thou art penniless and poor.
But were thou Master Masons,
    thou wouldst be rich for sure.

"For in my own country far away,
    the deed would soon be done.
We have need of Master Masons there.
    Wilt thou with me return?"

The Three Ruffians Conspire

These Fellow Craft did bow to hear,
    Queen Balkis order so.
But to their murderous task,
    they willingly did go.

And talking one to another,
    they could and did not see,
that Satan, the Devil himself,
    caused this evil to be.

"Ah, Jubela and Jubelum,
    why is knowledge given him?
Are we too not Masons here?
    That we know not is a sin!"

"Ah, Jubelo and Jubelum,
    I know not where we go.
But I too desire the knowledge,
    of a Master Mason so."

"Ah, Jubela and Jubelo
    my Fellows of the Craft.
Fear not for we soon shall have,
    the knowledge of his heart.

"But I pray thee both to think on this,
    is there so righteous a man,
as is this poor Widow's Son,
    in all God's, Glorious Land?

"Truly he is a man of God,
    let us not his work profane.
So let us but talk with him,
    and his Secrets we may yet gain."

The Three Ruffians Seek the Architect

So these three Fellow Craft,
    did seek the Widow's Son,
and meet him in the Temple grounds,
    when the day's work was done.

The prayer was said, the stars shone high,
    the moon shone ever on.
And so to bed would Hiram go,
    this pious Widow's Son.

"Oh Master Mason, most respected man,
    pray hear our earnest plea.
'Though we are but Fellow Craft,
    we would but speak with thee."

"Jubelo, I see," said the Widow's Son,
    "And Jubela and Jubelum.
What wouldst thou say to me this night?
    Come, walk with me. Come."

"Truly one Master Mason thou,
    and we but Fellow's three.
Many days have we laboured here,
    all for love of thee."

"We would not toil upon this land,
    for any here but thee.
So grant thou Master Mason,
    thy Secrets to us three."

"For we desire to leave this land,
 to earn much higher wages.
But how shall we alone do this,
 denied the Secrets Ageless?"

Hiram Abiff Answers the Three Ruffians

"Thou three serve not any man -
    thou dost the work of thy heart.
All Brethren here labour for God,
    to rest His Holy Ark.

"And God is with us in each day,
    He hears our every wish.
But in answer to thy request this day,
    hear thou all but this.

"Every man shall have his reward,
    every one in this land.
For the Lord our Only God above,
    shall protect us with His Hand.

"You have passed the Apprentice stage,
    and now are Fellows three.
Continue with thy honest endeavours,
    and the Secrets shall be given thee.

"But for the moment thou art Fellow Craft,
    labour thou honestly.
And soon thou shalt be Master Masons,
    and the Knowledge shall granted thee.

"Only three men do know the Word,
    for woman has all betrayed.
And 'though the Lord was verily angered,
    He has His Sword yet stayed.

"I am alone instructed by Him,
    in so many of life's ways.
And but to Him and Him alone,
    do I give thanks always.

"So now I bless thee Brethren all,
    with the Lord's Goodness and Will.
As thou have done His Work so far,
    I pray thee . . . do it still."

The Three Ruffians Depart

Then the Fellow Craft those three,
    they did all then depart.
And in the dead of that dark night,
    Satan entered their hearts.

Upon the morrow they did meet,
    these poor misguided three.
And in their midst Satan dwelt,
    'though him they could not see.

"Ah, Jubela and Jubelum,
    I could not sleep last night.
For in my dreams the Master's words,
    shone like the brightest light."

"Ah, Jubelo and Jubelum,
    I too could find no sleep.
For deep within my heart I cried,
    and Hiram's wish safe keep."

"Ah, Jubela and Jubelo,
    my brothers we are but three.
How shall we know the Mason Word?
    I ask this now of thee."

"My brothers, pray heed my voice,
    I know the path to take."
And so the Fellow Craft did hear,
    'though none of them spake.

"Soon the Master Mason,
  shall build a brazen sea.
And with thine aid my brothers here,
  surely there dies he."

So these poor misguided men,
  did speak to other men.
Three times four they swelled their ranks,
  and Satan appeared again.

The Brazen Sea

A mighty vessel soon was made,
    in which was melted brass.
So hot was the molten sea,
    it scorched the sand and grass.

In pouring of the burning brass,
    the Master was in command.
And as he would so often do,
    he stood upon the sand.

Upon the signal given there,
    one Fellow Craft did fall.
And as the burning metal fell,
    Hiram heard the Lord God call.

"Evil has entered into the hearts,
    of these poor Brethren three.
'Though Satan has turned their hearts,
    they shall not now harm thee."

And a mighty Angel stayed the sea;
    it fell upon dry ground.
And when the Brethren gathered there,
    the Widow's Son was found.

"Dear Brethren who are gathered here,
    pray hearken to my voice.
The Lord thy God is mighty indeed,
    so let us now rejoice.

"Satan himself cannot command,
    any heart pure and true.
So let us with the Temple's work,
    continue our efforts anew."

And all the Brethren gathered there,
    did wonder at this man.
For of all men the Lord God above,
    favoured him in that land.

Balkis Resolves to Kill the Widow's Son

In the Palace Queen Balkis sat,
    King Salomon by her side.
For the moment he did not know;
    in him she did not confide.

A messenger came sure and swift,
    to tell the joyous news.
That the Widow's only living Son,
    was saved by the One God True.

But Satan then was angered there,
    when his plans did go astray.
And so he vowed vengeance still,
    to triumph another day.

Balkis sat and heard the news,
    and feigned relief and mirth.
To hear the Widow's Son had died,
    she would gladly give the earth.

And Satan stood invisible there,
    and entered into her heart.
And secretly she vowed to tear,
    Hiram's body and soul apart.

Balkis Calls the Three Ruffians Again

To her Chamber Balkis then she called,
    the Fellow Craft three.
"Come! Come evil ones!
    I yet have need of thee!

"The Widow's Son yet does live,
    he has the Secrets still.
Come and hear my voice you three,
    come close and do my will.

"Soon the Temple will be complete,
    the Ark will be at peace.
If this should yet come to pass,
    all evil here shall cease.

"So act soon to do my will,
    and we shall kill this man.
That I alone shall rule this place,
    and I alone shall stand.

"Quick! Quick, it must be done!
    Hiram Abiff must die.
I must have the Secret Light,
    I see within his eyes.

"When his prayers this day are done,
    and he is all alone,
shall you Fellow Craft demand,
    secrets of a Master Mason.

"And when the evil deed is done,
    and his Knowledge then is mine.
I shall be the eternal ruler,
    for now and all time.

"Quick! Kill the Widow's son.
    Strike him with cold stone!
There in the Temple grounds,
    thou shalt find him quite alone."

The Fellow Craft Recant

So Satan entered there once more,
    into those Fellows' hearts.
And with those evil, wicked words,
    these three men did depart.

The other Fellow Craft did cower,
    when asked to kill this man.
"Surely the Lord our Only God,
    favours him in all this land?

"For who but God could have him saved,
    from that brazen sea?
Surely any who lifts his hand,
    shall be damned eternally!

"No, we shall not do this deed!
    We are but humble men.
What the Lord God alone has saved,
    we shall not kill again."

The Fellow Craft Inform King Salomon

Then those wise men twelve,
  being Fellows of the Craft,
they did to King Salomon go,
  to inform him of this act.

'Though the King received them there,
  he believed not their words.
For all the Brethren he did know,
  worked with tools, not swords.

And so the Fellow Craft twelve,
  returned at the King's behest.
For they were guided by their King,
  and thought no more of death.

Hiram Abiff Prays

At High Twelve did Hiram Abiff,
    pray once more to God.
But there in the Holy Temple,
    three Fellow Craft trod.

They watched the goodly Architect,
    as he knelt in humble prayer.
"Oh Lord, My God of Israel,
    thou dost dwell everywhere.

"And now I kneel before thee here,
    Thy Temple is all but complete.
Now Thine Ark shall rest in peace;
    I thank Thee for this feat.

"Thy Mighty Ark shall wander no more,
    hidden in veils and tents.
And now my Task is almost done,
    why must my life be rent?

"But I thank Thee that Thou has seen,
    fit still to hear my voice.
For in my service here to Thee,
    does my soul rejoice.

"I know the Task for which I came,
    is now all but done.
And soon I must leave the King,
    the Good King Salomon.

"Thy Will alone is mine to do,
 I shall where'er Thou Will.
As ever I have served Thee my Lord,
 I shall serve Thee ever still."

Hiram Abiff's Final Prayer

And so the Fellow Craft three,
    heard the Good Architect.
And quietly did they creep away,
    the Widow's Son they left.

By close of day the work was done,
    the Brethren all did sleep.
Only Hiram and the Fellow Craft,
    alone, awake did keep.

In duty to his belovèd God,
    Hiram prayed again.
He knelt there in the Lord's House,
    this most pious of all men.

"Oh Lord, My God of Israel,
    hear this Thy Servant's voice.
Guide me in this darkest hour,
    that in Thee I might rejoice.

"Thy Knowledge has made of me,
    mighty amongst all men.
But even so I come to thee,
    for Wisdom once again.

"Thy Holy Ark of the Covenant,
    will soon be laid at peace.
And with its rest in This Holy House,
    shall all evil here cease.

"For Thy Mighty Law for all Mankind,
    is held within the Ark.
And all men shall no more sin,
    if they hold it in their heart.

"But the Secrets of a Master Mason,
    Thou hast given unto me.
For with this Knowledge True and Pure,
    this Temple was built for Thee.

"I am a Master Mason,
    'though my blood within is stained.
For I am the humble, distant son,
    of the murderer Tubalcain.

"So grant me Thy Compassion,
    when I must leave this land.
For I know what must befall me here,
    at my fellow Mason's hand.

"The Secrets of a Master Mason,
    I have told to but two.
And these two men I devoutly trust,
    to keep Thine Secrets True.

"But the wisdom Thou hast given me,
    I have hidden in this place.
For none may know of it,
    as none may see Thine Face.

"So for my Master Masons two,
    have I left my final plans.
For they alone may complete,
    this Temple with their hands.

"Like unto Thy Servant Moses,
    alone I must dream this dream.
For this night I must away,
    I shall not live it seems.

"My weary eyes shall not behold,
    Thy Temple in all its glory.
For before this night is gone and done,
    shall be done a deed most gory.

"So pray my Lord, my only God,
    be ever by my side.
For this night I have need of strength;
    my soul with Thee abide.

"For my body now is old and weak,
    my only strength is Thee.
Upon this dark and bitter night,
    be Thou ever near with me."

The Heinous Deed is Done

The three Fellow Craft, those men,
    now moved to their positions.
With Satan deep in all their hearts,
    they were devoid of all compassion.

One hid at the Southern Gate,
    he yielded a single tool.
Within his murderous, evil hand,
    he held a great plumb-rule.

Another stood by the Western Gate,
    with a level in his hand.
And as he waited there alone,
    evil o'ertook this man.

The last he stood at the Eastern Gate,
    of the Sanctum Sanctorum Holy.
In his hand he had a setting maul,
    contemplating his deed most gory.

His prayer complete, Hiram arose,
    he bowed his final bow.
He turned around and would depart,
    the Lord's Will be done somehow.

The first of the Fellow Craft,
    stepped forth and grabbed his man.
He shook the Widow's only Son,
    a plumb-rule in his hand.

"Thou Architect of the land of Tyre,
    I am a desperate man!
Tell me the Secrets of a Master Mason,
    else I strike thee with this hand!"

"Thou poor misguided Fellow Craft,
    Jubelo is thine name.
Let the Lord God's Will be done,
    for our fate shall be the same.

"My life is but a temporal state;
    thou may it this night take.
But I shall ever to God be true,
    even for His own Name's sake.

"The Secrets of a Master Mason,
    are known to but a few.
'Though my life you may well take,
    this I shall not tell you."

"So be it," then cried Jubelo,
    and struck him a mighty blow.
With blood trailing from his left temple,
    to the West Gate did he go.

There the second Fellow Craft,
    stepped forth and grabbed his man.
He shook the Widow's only Son,
    brandishing a level in his hand.

"Thou Architect of the land of Tyre,
    I am a desperate man!
Tell me the Secrets of a Master Mason,
    else I strike thee with this hand!"

"Thou poor misguided Fellow Craft,
    Jubela is thine name.
Let the Lord God's Will be done,
    for our fate shall be the same.

"My life is but a temporal state;
    thou may it this night take.
But I shall ever to God be true,
    even for His own Name's sake.

"The Secrets of a Master Mason,
    are known to but a few.
'Though my life you may well take,
    this I shall not tell you."

"So be it!" then cried Jubela,
    and struck him a mighty blow.
With blood trailing from his right temple,
    to the East Gate he then did go.

There the third Fellow Craft,
    stepped forth and grabbed his man.
He shook the Widow's only Son,
    a setting maul in his hand.

"Thou Architect of the land of Tyre,
  I am a desperate man!
Tell me the Secrets of a Master Mason,
  else I strike thee with this hand!"

"Thou poor misguided Fellow Craft,
  Jubelum is thine name.
Let the Lord God's Will be done,
  for our fate shall be the same.

"My life is but a temporal state;
  thou may it this night take.
But I shall ever to God be true,
  even for His own Name's sake.

"The Secrets of a Master Mason,
  are known to but a few.
'Though my life you might well take,
  this I shall not tell you."

"So be it!" then cried Jubelum,
  and struck him a mighty blow.
With blood trailing from his head,
  to his death did Hiram go.

"My Lord God of Israel,
  look down from Heaven above.
Pray have mercy on these Fellow Craft;
  grant them Eternal Love.

"For they know not what they do,
    upon this dark, bitter night.
Pray let Thy Will be done.
    guide them to Thy Light."

And so the heinous deed was done;
    the Architect lay dead.
And there upon that Holy Ground,
    blood flowed from his head.

The Widow's Son is Dead

Now the Fellow Craft did look,
    those poor unfortunate three.
And from their wicked, evil deed,
    would they all then flee.

They gathered the lifeless body,
    and laid it amongst the stone.
And there that dark and bitter night,
    the Architect lay alone.

Later they did all three return,
    and the rubble they laid aside.
For there near the keystone,
    did they the body hide.

And taking up his body,
    they carried the Widow's Son.
And by the light of the moon above,
    their evil act was done.

They travelled beyond the Temple,
    when they came to virgin ground.
And there by Mount Moriah,
    they cast the body down.

There in the sun-baked, barren ground,
    they dug a shallow grave.
And there they laid the body down,
    for they would their own lives save.

No prayers were said for him,
    the dead man lay alone.
There was no mark to mark him there,
    no flowers nor gravestone.

A Sprig of Acacia

But Jubelum did then repent,
    of the deed which he had done.
And sought to mark his Master's grave,
    with a single, solitary stone.

But no stone could there be found,
    but only an Acacia tree.
He marked the grave with a sprig thereof,
    then from that place did flee.

Confusion at the Temple

To the Temple all the Brethren came,
    to commence the final task.
But no sight was there of the Grand Master,
    so of Salomon did they ask.

"Pray tell us of his whereabouts,
    for our task cannot be done.
For Hiram Abiff has the final plans;
    the Widow's only Son.

"We are but Entered Apprentices,
    and Fellows of the Craft.
We cannot work without our Master,
    so for him do we now ask.

"It is his daily custom,
    to rise and be at prayer.
But waking from our beds this morn,
    we did not see him there.

"And daily would he ever,
    as ever he was true,
leave instructions on the tressle board,
    of the tasks that we must do.

"But these are not here laid down,
    as would be the Master's task.
And so in fear and trembling,
    do we of you now ask.

"We know not where he might be,
    for his life we now do fear.
So to thee our King Salomon,
    do we now come here."

King Salomon Fears for the Widow's Son

"I know not of the Widow's Son.
    or of aught where he may be.
But when I consider thee all,
    thy numbers are all but three.

"Where are the Fellow Craft,
    whom I saw not long ago?
For where the Architect may be,
    I fear they alone may know.

"Swift! Swift! Call them here,
    those Fellow Craft men three.
And truly I shall ask of them,
    where our Brother might yet be."

So all the Brethren gathered there,
    now sought the Fellows three.
But nowhere could they be found,
    none knew where they might be.

Salomon then to the Temple came,
    and there found Hiram's blood.
He came in fear before the Ark,
    before the Lord he stood.

"My Lord, My God of Israel,
    Thou art most Good and Kind.
Pray hear thy servant here and now,
    the Architect I would find."

The Lord then spake to Salomon,
    the trail of blood to follow.
At the end of that gory track,
    will be the Son of the Widow.

To the South Gate first he went,
    and thence to the West Gate also.
But then the trail of blood led on;
    to the East Gate he did follow.

From there all the Brethren went,
    to the waste and rubble ground.
And there amongst the broken stones,
    yet more blood they found.

"I fear for the Widow's Son,
    I fear that he is dead.
For this must be his precious blood,
    spilled from his precious head.

"But look! Yonder the blood leads on;
    let us follow it still more.
For I fear we shall find him there,
    in a pool of mud and gore.

"I must bear a heavy burden,
    so heavy in my heart.
For I would not heed their warning,
    and bid twelve Fellows depart."

King Salomon Orders a Search

"Ye goodly men, ye Fellow Craft,
    pray continue with this task.
For I must to our Lord God pray,
    and again His Aid ask.

"And this too I do ask of thee,
    ride the winds swiftly.
Search for those Fellow Craft three,
    and bring them here to me."

And then those goodly Fellow Craft,
    went to that desert ground.
But 'though they looked here and there,
    the body could not be found.

The Three Ruffians Flee

Jubelo, Jubela and Jubelum,
    raced fast across the sand.
Their one intent was to escape,
    their Brethren in that land.

At dead of night they gathered round,
    a small and still camp fire,
that sent small, starry, sparks,
    into the air and higher.

Each one of them was deeply troubled;
    no rest could they find.
For 'though Satan dwelt with them,
    still guilt wracked their minds.

They made their way to Joppa;
    for Ethiopia they hoped.
But while they waited for a ship to sail,
    to none other they spoke.

They three hid inside a cave,
    and drank a bitter brew.
And there in that desolate place,
    they spoke their minds true.

Then Satan abandoned them,
    to pay the price of sin.
Now that his task was done,
    he left them empty within.

"Ah Jubela, my poor desperate brother.
    I would that God were near.
I would that I had killed him not,
    that we might not be here.

"For I struck him on the head;
    how his blood did flow!
And laughing then, there at him,
    I watched him fall and go."

"Ah Jubelum, my poor desperate brother,
    I would that God were here.
I would that I had killed him not,
    that our Master might be here.

"I too struck him on the head;
    how his blood did flow!
And laughing then, there at him,
    I watched him fall and go."

"Ah Jubelo, my poor desperate brother.
    I wish that God were near.
I would that I had killed him not,
    that he might still be here.

"For I too struck him a mighty blow;
    how his blood did flow!
And laughing then, there at him,
    I watched him fall below.

"And more than this I heard him fall,
    down to his bare knees.
I heard him pray to God above,
    'though I would not hear his plea."

The Self-Imposed Penalties

Then guilt-wracked Jubelo he cried;
    he cried such bitter tears.
"I would my throat be cut across,
    from one to other ear.

"This punishment I would gladly bear,
    so dearly I would embrace.
If by my own, my untimely death,
    I could see my Master's face."

Then guilt-wracked Jubela too he cried;
    for his soul was rent apart.
"I would my breast be torn asunder,
    and therefrom plucked my heart.

"Then let it be cast away,
    over my right shoulder.
And there in the desert lay,
    upon a sun-burned boulder.

"For I too, I too am guilty,
    of taking his good life.
And evermore shall I rightly suffer,
    torment and strife."

Then Jubelum too he cried;
    his body and soul were pained.
"I would my belly be cut thus,
    and therefrom torn my entrails.

"Then cast them in the desert heat,
    to feed the fowl of the air.
This I would so gladly do,
    to see my Master fair."

The Ruffians Captured

And so King Salomon's men,
    rode on and to and fro.
To all the ports of that good land,
    did they with all haste go.

Some travelled to the North,
    but nothing did they discover.
And so back to Jerusalem,
    returned these goodly Brothers.

Others did to the East and South;
    they travelled with great haste.
But nowhere did they the ruffians find,
    these goodly Brothers chaste.

Still more to the West did go,
    in answer to Royal Command.
And diligently did each one of them,
    search throughout that land.

They came at last to Joppa port,
    and heard of strangers three.
And continuing their searches there,
    they looked most diligently.

They came unto a small, dark cave,
    and heard great lamentation.
And there they did all stay,
    in horrified contemplation.

They could bear to hear no more,
    and entered into that place.
They held those wicked ruffians three,
    and returned to Salomon's palace.

Mount Moriah's Secret

"Let us now here stop a while,
    and rest our weary heads.
For the sun is bright above us here,"
    one worthy Brother said.

And so the Brethren rested there,
    and held their weary heads.
All did pray to God above,
    that their Master might not be dead.

Then rising from his short rest,
    a Brother rose in prayer.
"My Lord, My God of Israel,
    show me my Master fair."

He placed his hand upon a sprig,
    an Acacia plant he plucked.
And there to his great surprise,
    he found it was not stuck.

Then he looked a little closer;
    the earth was fresh around.
And as he dug deeper still,
    he feared what might be found.

"Worthy Brethren! Come, hurry here.
    I fear what I have found.
For the earth here disturbèd is;
    come look upon this ground.

"Let us now haste to our King,
    and bring news to mount Moriah.
And let us also kneel in prayer,
    that we have our heart's desire."

The Widow's Son Discovered

Salomon came to that place,
    and saw with his own eyes.
Looking at the shallow grave,
    he raised his hands on high.

"My Lord, My God of Israel,
    let this Thy Will be done.
If it be thy pleasure here and now,
    grant me the Widow's Son."

"Good Brother come," said Salomon.
    "Wilt thou dig a little more?
With God's Good Grace from Heaven above,
    we may our Brother restore.

"Here! Here! Here is the grave,
    that inters our dear Grand Master.
Pray dig thee still most carefully,
    but dig thou still faster."

The grave was six by six and feet three,
    as dug the Fellow Craft.
And diligently did these Brothers,
    as their worthy King had asked.

The body of the Grand Master,
    was thus discovered there.
And all who saw that dread sight,
    fell back in despair.

King Salomon too did weep to see,
    and gave the sign of distress.
As he looked upon the Widow's Son,
    the Brethren felt helpless.

Attempts to Raise the Widow's Son

"My worthy Junior Warden,
    pray descend into this grave.
And with the grip of an Entered Apprentice,
    our Master's body raise."

But the Worthy Junior Warden,
    try as he well might.
He could not raise the body,
    and turned from that dread sight.

"My Worthy Master and my King,
    verily it proves the slip.
'Though an Entered Apprentice's grip I gave,
    still, I cannot raise it."

"Alas! Alas! Alas!"
    All worthy Brethren cried.
"Is there no help for the Widow's Son,
    now that he has died?"

"My worthy Senior Warden,
    pray descend into this grave.
And with the grip of a Fellow Craft,
    our Master's body raise."

But the Worthy Senior Warden,
    try as he well might,
he could not raise the body,
    and turned from that dread sight.

"My Worthy Master and my King,
   verily it proves the slip.
'Though a Fellow Craft's grip I gave,
   still I cannot raise it."

"Alas! Alas! Alas!"
   all worthy Brethren cried.
"Is there no help for the Widow's Son,
   now that he has died?"

"Naught is left but for me to try,"
   King Salomon then he said.
"I shall with the Lion's claw,
   attempt to raise the dead."

And so the King himself went down,
   into that deathly grave,
and with the grip of a Master Mason,
   the Master's soul was saved.

The body then was raised on high,
   and returned to Jerusalem.
And there the Temple was made whole,
   by the worthy Brethren.

King Salomon then cast down,
   a mighty pillar great,
in remembrance of the Widow's Son,
   whose life he could not save.

Punishment for the Guilty

King Salomon passed judgement,
    on all that did conspire.
But first he bowed his head in prayer,
    seeking guidance from on High.

The ruffians were before him brought;
    they confessed their every sin.
And so Salomon passed the sentences,
    they uttered the cave within.

The Queen of Sheba too was brought,
    to face the mighty King.
But he loved her so within his heart,
    he took from her his ring.

"Thou art, my love, of Royal blood,
    and thou hast won my heart.
But for this sin of yours and mine,
    we must now ever part.

"The Widow and her only Son,
    now, they are no more.
And I must share this sorrow here,
    and cast thou me before.

"Thou hast defiled the Good Lord's Land,
    and brought on us disgrace.
So now I bid thee leave my land,
    And ne'er show thy face."

And so the Queen, Balkis left,
    but a son was in her womb.
And so a life would soon replace,
    one laid inside a tomb.

And in the coming years and time,
    the Ark would be away.
And the people and King Salomon,
    would from the Lord God stray.

But the Lord our God is Good and Kind;
    He is but only One.
In years to come, He would return,
    the Widow's Everlasting Son.

www.ingramcontent.com/pod-product-compliance
Lightning Source LLC
Chambersburg PA
CBHW071140090426
42736CB00012B/2174